THE HEIDEGGER DICTIONARY

ISAAC VOLPE

THE HEIDEGGER DICTIONARY

An Examination of His Key Concepts and Terms

© 2023 by Isaac Volpe
© 2023 by UNITEXTO
All rights reserved

Published by UNITEXTO

THE HEIDEGGER DICTIONARY
An Examination of His Key Concepts and Terms

TABLE OF CONTENTS

Why this book?
Martin Heidegger: A short bio
About the author
Key Concepts and Terms
    Anxiety (Angst)
    Anxiety towards death
    Art (Kunst)
    Authentic existence
    Authenticity
    Awaiting (Erwarten)
    Being (Sein)
    Being-in (Insein)
    Being-in-the-future (Zukünftigkeit)
    Being-in-the-past (Vergangenheit)
    Being-in-the-world (In-der-Welt-sein)
    Being-there (Da-sein)
    Being-towards-death (Sein-zum-Tode)
    Being-toward-the-world (In-der-Welt-Sein)
    Being-with (Mitdasein)
    Being-with-one-another (Miteinandersein)
    Being-with-others (Mitsein)
    Being-with-others (Mitsein)
    Care (Sorge)
    Care for the self
    Care structure
    Circumspection (Umsicht)
    Clearing (Lichtung)

Conceptual framework (Begriffliche Rahmung)
Conceptualization (Begriff)
Conscience (Gewissen)
Consciousness (Bewusstsein)
Da-sein
Dasein (Existence)
Death (Tod)
Deathlessness (Todlosigkeit)
De-severance (Entzweiung)
Disclosure (Erschlossenheit)
Distantiality (Entfernung)
Dwelling (Wohnen)
Essence (Wesen)
Essence and existence
Event (Ereignis)
Eventfulness (Ereignishaftigkeit)
Existential
Existential analytic
Existentialism
Experiencing (Erleben)
Facticity (Faktizität)
Finitude
Freedom (Freiheit)
Geist (Spirit)
Geschichte (History)
Geworfenheit (thrownness)
Ground (Grund)
Guilt (Schuld)
Hermeneutics
Historicity
Humanism
Identity (Identität)
Inauthenticity
Interpretation
Language (Sprache)
Language game (Sprachspiel)

Meaning (Bedeutung)
Metaphysics
Mitdasein (being-with)
Mortality (Sterblichkeit)
Nothingness (Nichts)
Ontic
Ontological difference
Ontology
Openness (Offenheit)
Otherness (Andersheit)
Phenomenology
Phenomenon (Phänomen)
Pre-reflective understanding
Projection (Entwurf)
Reality (Realität)
Resoluteness (Entschlossenheit)
Self (Selbst)
Selfhood (Selbstsein)
Silence (Schweigen)
Temporal ecstases
Temporality
Temporality (Temporalität)
Temporality (Zeitlichkeit)
The they (Das Man)
Thing (Ding)
Thinking (Denken)
Thrownness (Geworfenheit)
Time (Zeit)
Tradition (Tradition)
Truth (Wahrheit)
Unconcealment (Unverborgenheit)
Understanding (Verstehen)
Uniqueness (Einzigkeit)
Untruth (Unwahrheit)
Verfallen (falling prey)
Vorhanden (present-at-hand)

Welt (World)
Work of art (Kunstwerk)
World-disclosure (Welterschlossenheit)
Worldhood (Weltlichkeit)
Worldliness (Weltlichkeit)

Why this book?

Why this book, you may ask? Why take on the Herculean task of unraveling the complex vocabulary and profound concepts of Martin Heidegger, one of the most influential philosophers of the 20th century?

The answer lies in the power of language and the transformational journey it invites us on when we truly engage with it. Martin Heidegger's work, with its intricate and thought-provoking ideas, epitomizes this transformative potential. However, the depth and complexity of his language often pose an obstacle to the reader's understanding.

It is with the aim of bridging this gap and fostering a deeper comprehension of Heidegger's ideas that "THE HEIDEGGER DICTIONARY: An Examination of His Key Concepts and Terms" was conceived.

This book is more than just a dictionary; it is a compendium of Heidegger's philosophical landscape. It meticulously curates the 100 most fundamental concepts in Heidegger's philosophy, providing each term with a detailed explanation and accompanying it with direct quotations from Heidegger's works, thereby placing them in their appropriate intellectual contexts.

It is a navigational tool, designed to guide you through the labyrinthine corridors of Heidegger's thought, illuminating his ideas and helping you forge your path.

"THE HEIDEGGER DICTIONARY" is for the curious, the thinkers, and the seekers. It is for students grappling with the intricacies of Heidegger's philosophy and for the lay reader attempting to comprehend his existential and phenomenological ideas. It is for anyone who wishes to venture into the philosophical realm of Heidegger, gain insights into his profound vocabulary, and explore his transformative ideas.

In these pages, you will find more than definitions; you will find a means to engage more deeply with one of the most complex minds in the history of philosophy. This book invites you to step beyond the surface, to engage with Heidegger's thought in a deeper, more meaningful way, and to embark on your own philosophical journey.

Why this book? Because understanding Heidegger's philosophy is about more than mere intellectual curiosity—it's about exploring the depth of our existence and the world we inhabit. And so we invite you to delve into "THE HEIDEGGER DICTIONARY," a stepping stone into the extraordinary philosophical realm of Martin Heidegger.

Here you will find five reasons to read this book:

1. **Unravel the Complexity**
   : Martin Heidegger's philosophy is renowned for its profound depth and complexity. Reading "THE HEIDEGGER DICTIONARY: An Examination of His Key Concepts and Terms" will help you decode his intricate ideas, providing an accessible pathway into his philosophical world.
2. **Deepen Your Understanding**
   If you're a student, a scholar of philosophy, or just someone interested in philosophical thought, this book will serve as an invaluable tool, enriching your knowledge and deepening your understanding of Heidegger's theories and concepts.
3. **Engage with Primary Text:**

The book doesn't merely define terms; it uses quotations from Heidegger's works to place each concept in its appropriate context. This makes the dictionary a fantastic companion when reading Heidegger's original texts, helping you to understand and engage with his writings at a deeper level.

4. **Intellectual Expansion:**
   Heidegger's philosophy offers profound insights into the nature of being, time, and the human condition. By reading this book, you're embarking on an intellectual journey that will expand your perspectives and potentially transform the way you view yourself and the world.

5. **Practical Resource:**
   As a handy, comprehensive, and meticulously researched guide, "THE HEIDEGGER DICTIONARY" serves as a useful resource, whether you're writing a paper, preparing for a lecture, or just satisfying your intellectual curiosity. It's a tool you'll find yourself reaching for whenever you want to dive deeper into Heidegger's world.

Isaac Volpe

Martin Heidegger: A Short Bio

Martin Heidegger (1889–1976) was a German philosopher whose work is considered seminal in the fields of existentialism, phenomenology, and hermeneutics. One of the most influential philosophers of the 20th century, his ideas have had a profound impact across various disciplines, including philosophy, theology, psychology, and literary theory.

Heidegger was born in the town of Meßkirch, Germany. He initially studied for the priesthood and even spent some time in a Jesuit seminary before switching his focus to philosophy. He completed his doctoral thesis on psychologies, inspired by neo-Thomism and the works of Franz Brentano and Edmund Husserl.

His early academic career was significantly shaped by his mentorship under Husserl, the founder of phenomenology. However, Heidegger soon developed his philosophical approach that diverged from Husserl's, placing a greater emphasis on 'Being'.

Heidegger's best-known book, "Being and Time" ("Sein und Zeit"), published in 1927, is considered his most significant work. It delves into the concept of 'Being', exploring the relationship between the temporal and ontological aspects of human existence. The book introduced the term "Dasein" to describe the nature of being in the world.

Despite his contributions to philosophy, Heidegger's reputation has been clouded by his association with the Nazi Party. He joined the party in 1933 and served as the rector of Freiburg University, where he implemented Nazi policies. However, he resigned from the rectorship within a year due to political conflicts.

In his later years, Heidegger distanced himself from existentialist thought and shifted his focus towards language, technology, and art. His later works inspired postmodernist thinkers like Jacques Derrida and Michel Foucault. Despite the controversy surrounding his political affiliations, Heidegger's philosophical insights continue to be highly influential in the field of contemporary philosophy.

About the Author

Isaac Volpe: An Intellect in the Interwoven Worlds of History and Philosophy

Born in Lithuania in 1973, Isaac Volpe has spent the last half-century on an intellectual odyssey, exploring the vast territories of history and philosophy, dissecting their complexities, and revealing their intriguing intersections. At the heart of his journey lies a persistent curiosity and dedication to learning, the seeds of which were sown during his formative years in Eastern Europe.

Educated initially in his home country, Isaac's academic talents propelled him westward to the prestigious halls of La Sorbonne in Paris, France. It was there, under the tutelage of renowned academics, where he honed his skills and cultivated his interests in the disciplines that would shape his career. Graduating with distinction, he demonstrated an impressive grasp of intricate philosophical concepts and historical epochs.

Isaac's subsequent research and publications have illuminated his exceptional ability to shed new light on familiar topics. He stands out for his ability to intertwine historical events and philosophical notions, creating a unique blend of scholarly investigation that has consistently challenged traditional academic boundaries.

His work, characterized by rigorous analyses and eloquent prose, showcases his comprehensive knowledge of both disciplines. From exploring the impact of existentialist thought on post-war Europe to delving into the philosophical underpinnings of the Renaissance, Isaac has proved to be a gifted thinker and storyteller.

Beyond his scholarly accomplishments, Isaac is known for his empathetic nature and engaging teaching style. His commitment to education has inspired countless students to delve deeper into the realms of history and philosophy, with many citing his enthusiasm and broad knowledge as key motivators in their own academic journeys.

As he enters his 50s, Isaac Volpe remains as curious and passionate as ever. Through his significant contributions and continuous dedication to his fields of interest, he embodies the rare combination of a profound scholar and a passionate educator. It is this ceaseless curiosity and the delight he takes in sharing his knowledge that makes Isaac such an inspiration to all who cross his path.

IsaacVolpe

Key Concepts and Terms

1. Anxiety (Angst):

Definition:
Anxiety in Heidegger's philosophy refers to a fundamental mood or existential condition, often characterized by a sense of unease, dread, or angst. It is not merely a psychological state but an essential aspect of human existence, revealing our finitude and the uncertainties of life.

Quotations:

- "Anxiety reveals the nothing. Anxiety is the mood in which that which is close and not-to-hand, as something, becomes most distant. The nothing threatens, but in such a way that it is precisely the nothing in which everything stands, the nothing in which everything rests, and so it is the nothing that threatens." (From "What is Metaphysics?")

- "Anxiety is the basic mood of Dasein itself in its everyday being, but still, it is only one of the possibilities of this being." (From "Being and Time")

- "Anxiety makes manifest the Nothing. The world and beings as a whole sink away in the face of the Nothing. It becomes known in anxiety that the 'world' as world is held together only by human being. The world emerges as world only when it is discovered and disclosed by human being as world." (From "Introduction to Metaphysics")

2. Anxiety towards death:

Definition:

Anxiety towards death refers to the existential angst and unease experienced when confronting the inevitability of one's mortality. It is not merely the fear of physical death but an awareness of the finitude and transitory nature of human existence.

Quotations:

- "In anxiety, Dasein has its uncanniest and most obvious possibility of being itself, primarily not in its exteriority to something else but in its Being-in-the-world with this Something. In anxiety, the nothing is manifest in the fact that the 'world' comes to Dasein as a whole." (From "Being and Time")

- "Dread of death is not simply anxiety in the face of an end, a threat of annihilation, but anxiety as regards the potentiality-for-Being of one's own most being. This means that we must understand authentic anxiety as Angst in the face of death." (From "Basic Concepts")

- "The dread of death reveals itself essentially as Angst in the face of one's ownmost potentiality-for-Being, which is non-relational, and so reveals the groundlessness of Dasein in its thrownness." (From "Being and Time")

3. Art (Kunst):

Definition:
Art, in Heidegger's philosophy, goes beyond mere aesthetics and refers to the process of revealing and bringing forth truth and the essence of beings. Art is a fundamental way through which human beings encounter and understand the world.

Quotations:

- "The poet's word is a bringing to language of the Being of entities—their Being brought to language. This bringing to language is accomplished through the fact that in the word that which is, the world of entities, emerges and continues to emerge." (From "The Origin of the Work of Art")

- "The artist's vocation is to create the stage on which the truth is performed." (From "The Question Concerning Technology")

- "Art is the setting-into-work of truth. As such, art is in itself a happening of Being." (From "Basic Concepts")

4. Authentic existence:

Definition:
Authentic existence, according to Heidegger, is the mode of being in which an individual takes responsibility for their existence and lives genuinely, acknowledging their finitude, freedom, and the call of conscience.

Quotations:

- "Dasein is as it can be, and always only to the extent that it has been. It is its past in the way it has been, and it has been as its future 'is,' or as it may be." (From "Being and Time")

- "Resoluteness is the anticipation of death as a possibility of the uttermost impossibility of Dasein. In resoluteness, Dasein discloses itself to itself as resolute." (From "Being and Time")

- "The Self that has been lost in the 'They' [the everyday public world] is found again in resolute Being-toward-death." (From "Being and Time")

5. Authenticity:

Definition:
Authenticity in Heideggerian terms refers to the state of living an individual's life authentically, owning up to one's existence, and taking responsibility for the choices and possibilities inherent in human existence.

Quotations:

- "The authenticity of anxiety lies in Dasein's being open for its ownmost potentiality-for-Being. Anxiety individualizes, and it individualizes by disclosing the most potentiality-for-Being of Dasein." (From "Being and Time")

- "The 'They,' which supplies Dasein with its possibilities of interpreting itself, has ascribed to 'resoluteness' the character of defiance and waywardness. In point of fact, however, resoluteness is the most authentic and 'disciplined' Being-one's-Self." (From "Being and Time")

- "Authenticity means to exist in such a way that one's being-toward-death does not remain concealed but comes to light." (From "Being and Time")

6. Awaiting (Erwarten):

Definition:
Awaiting, in Heidegger's thought, is the existential state of being open to the possibilities that the future may bring. It involves a sense of anticipation and receptivity to what is yet to come.

Quotations:

- "To await something means: to expect it in such a way that one is open and accessible for it." (From "Basic Concepts")

- "To await means: to be ready and open to the occurrence of something." (From "Basic Concepts")

- "To be able to await is a necessity for every openness in the face of beings and for every encounter with them." (From "Basic Concepts")

7. Being (Sein):

Definition:
Being (Sein) is a central concept in Heidegger's philosophy, representing the fundamental nature of existence, the ground of all beings, and the source of their intelligibility.

Quotations:

- "Being is the most universal concept." (From "Basic Concepts")

- "Being is not something like a being; it is neither an entity nor an ens, nor a being." (From "Basic Concepts")

- "Being is, as the ground of all grounds, that which first makes possible the manifestation of beings." (From "Basic Concepts")

8. Being-in (Insein):

Definition:
Being-in (Insein) is a term in Heidegger's philosophy that signifies the mode of existence in which Dasein (human being) is

inherently situated within a world and engaged with its environment and others.

Quotations:

- "Being-in is the basic state of Dasein. It is that state of Dasein which we have chosen as our theme for investigation." (From "Being and Time")

- "Being-in is a structural whole, and as such, it is constituted by the unity of those items which we have distinguished as constitutive for it." (From "Being and Time")

- "Being-in does not signify a spatial 'in' which is just

around things. It signifies being outside in the sense of 'seeing something.'" (From "Basic Concepts")

9. Being-in-the-future (Zukünftigkeit):

Definition:
Being-in-the-future refers to the existential mode in which human existence is characterized by its potentiality and openness towards the future. It involves a projection towards possibilities that lie ahead.

Quotations:

- "The anticipation of something, in a concern, makes the future 'present at hand' in a definite way. It is as this that Dasein is 'with' the 'world' toward which it is projected." (From "Being and Time")

- "Anticipation has disclosed to Dasein its Being towards its ownmost potentiality-for-Being, and has done so in terms of its uttermost possibility." (From "Being and Time")

- "The future, as the mode of Being of the future disclosed in anxiety, is the future of the disclosedness of entities in the clearing of Being." (From "Basic Concepts")

10. Being-in-the-past (Vergangenheit):

Definition:
Being-in-the-past refers to the existential mode in which human existence is connected to its past, shaped by its history, and influenced by past experiences.

Quotations:

- "That which has been in the past is itself something present." (From "Basic Concepts")

- "The future can reach only that which is able to be affected by entities which have been and are." (From "Basic Concepts")

- "The past of the understanding as the 'having-been-there' (Gewesensein) is neither earlier nor later than its future, but both lie before Dasein in such a way that it is open for them." (From "Basic Concepts")

11. Being-in-the-world (In-der-Welt-sein):

Definition:
Being-in-the-world signifies the inseparable interconnectedness of human existence (Dasein) with the world, implying that we do

not exist as isolated individuals but always in relation to the world we inhabit.

Quotations:

- "Being-in is, as we have shown, a constitutive existential of Dasein. This does not signify that it is a kind of being of Dasein, but rather that it is a way in which Dasein is." (From "Being and Time")

- "Dasein is Being-in-the-world, but never as a mere part of the totality of entities. Dasein does not just occur in the world; rather, it is ontically distinguished by the world." (From "Being and Time")

- "The world is essentially discovered, not only as the one that can be physically surrounded, but as the one that can be taken care of." (From "Being and Time")

12. Being-there (Da-sein):

Definition:
Being-there (Da-sein) is a term used by Heidegger to refer to human existence, emphasizing the notion that humans are not just entities present in the world but actively involved in understanding and engaging with the world.

Quotations:

- "Dasein does not just occur in the world; rather, it is ontically distinguished by the world. The primary phenomenon of Being-in is Being-in-the-world." (From "Being and Time")

- "Dasein's Being is essentially Being-in, which is to say that in its very Being, it is essentially directed toward its Being." (From "Basic Concepts")

- "The Being of Dasein must itself be exhibited in its whole structure." (From "Being and Time")

13. Being-towards-death (Sein-zum-Tode):

Definition:
Being-towards-death refers to the existential mode in which human existence is characterized by its awareness of mortality, leading to a profound sense of anxiety and a call for authentic living.

Quotations:

- "In the anticipation of death, Dasein is most authentically itself; indeed, this anticipation is what constitutes its authenticity." (From "Being and Time")

- "As Being-in-the-world, and as existing factically within the world, Dasein is essentially open for death. Dasein is, in its very Being, something that does not just 'have' its death, but has it as a possibility of its Being." (From "Being and Time")

- "Death, as something still outstanding, is Dasein's ownmost potentiality-for-Being." (From "Basic Concepts")

14. Being-toward-the-world (In-der-Welt-Sein):

Definition:

Being-toward-the-world signifies the directedness of human existence (Dasein) towards the world. It refers to the inherent nature of humans to relate to and understand the world in which they exist.

Quotations:

- "The essence of Dasein lies in its Being directed towards its ownmost potentiality-for-Being." (From "Being and Time")

- "The fact that Dasein is 'in-the-world' expresses in itself, ontologically, the primordial existential unity of these structures." (From "Being and Time")

- "Being-in-the-world means that Dasein, with its own way of Being, is 'in the truth of Being'." (From "Basic Concepts")

15. Being-with (Mitdasein):

Definition:
Being-with (Mitdasein) refers to the existential condition of human existence as being inherently related to and connected with others. It highlights the essential sociality and coexistence of humans.

Quotations:

- "Being-with signifies Being alongside entities which are encountered within-the-world; it implies an existential possibility of Being as such and in a way that this possibility is one's own." (From "Being and Time")

- "The Being of Dasein has Being-with-one-another as a kind of Being with itself." (From "Being and Time")

- "Dasein as being-in-the-world is, in each case, in-the-world alongside entities which it encounters." (From "Being and Time")

16. Being-with-one-another (Miteinandersein):

Definition:
Being-with-one-another (Miteinandersein) denotes the interconnectedness and coexistence of human beings in a shared world. It highlights the social dimension of human existence.

Quotations:

- "Being-with-one-another as the disclosedness of entities in the clearing of Being is the Being of Da-sein." (From "Basic Concepts")

- "Being-with-one-another does not signify a sum of persons present-at-hand. The entities are with one another in such a way that they first belong to one another as entities within-the-world." (From "Basic Concepts")

- "The Others with whom one is authentically concerned in a social way have the primordial kind of Being with which one is concernfully involved as Being-with." (From "Basic Concepts")

17. Being-with-others (Mitsein):

Definition:
Being-with-others (Mitsein) refers to the existential condition of human existence as being always alongside and interconnected with other human beings. It emphasizes the essential communal nature of being.

Quotations:

- "Being-with, however, is not an aggregate of isolated co-present individuals. Dasein, by its very Being, is Being-with." (From "Being and Time")

- "The phenomenon of the 'they' is one of the existentialia of the 'there' (Da) of Dasein." (From "Being and Time")

- "The Others with whom one is authentically concerned in a social way have the primordial kind of Being with which one is concernfully involved as Being-with." (From "Basic Concepts")

18. Being-with-others (Mitsein):

Definition:
Being-with-others (Mitsein) refers to the existential condition of human existence as being always alongside and interconnected with other human beings. It emphasizes the essential communal nature of being.

Quotations:

- "Being-with, however, is not an aggregate of isolated co-present individuals. Dasein, by its very Being, is Being-with." (From "Being and Time")

- "The phenomenon of the 'they' is one of the existentialia of the 'there' (Da) of Dasein." (From "Being and Time")

- "The Others with whom one is authentically concerned in a social way have the primordial kind of Being with which one is concernfully involved as Being-with." (From "Basic Concepts")

19. Care (Sorge):

Definition:
Care (Sorge) is a fundamental existential structure of human existence in which Dasein is always concerned with its possibilities, its world, and its own being. It involves both solicitude and concern.

Quotations:

- "Care is not a property of Dasein but its most being as such." (From "Being and Time")

- "Care is the basic way in which Dasein, essentially and as a whole, is in each case." (From "Being and Time")

- "Care makes things conspicuous; it brings along concern, and it keeps Dasein from getting out of the existing whole into isolated items." (From "Being and Time")

20. Care for the self:

Definition:
Care for the self-denotes the aspect of human existence that involves taking responsibility for one's own life, well-being, and self-understanding.

Quotations:

- "In the certainty of Dasein's death, Dasein gains itself, and therewith, its own ability-to-be as an ability-to-be-for-the-whole-of-its-being." (From "Being and Time")

- "The self that has been lost in the 'they' [the everyday public world] is found again in resolute Being-toward-death." (From "Being and Time")

- "The mineness of Dasein's being revealed in anxiety brings Dasein face to face with its authentic self." (From "Basic Concepts")

21. Care structure:

Definition:
Care structure refers to the fundamental framework of human existence, characterized by Dasein's interconnectedness with the world, its possibilities, and its own being. It constitutes the foundation of Dasein's existence.

Quotations:

- "The Being of Dasein is such that it understands itself and interprets itself in terms of its own most potentiality-for-Being." (From "Being and Time")

- "Care structures the Being of Dasein with regard to its being as a whole." (From "Basic Concepts")

- "The totality of the existentialia which have been exhibited by our analysis in each case makes up a unified whole, which we call the care structure." (From "Being and Time")

22. Circumspection (Umsicht):

Definition:

Circumspection (Umsicht) refers to the existential mode in which Dasein is always circumspect or attentive towards its surroundings and the entities within its environment.

Quotations:

- "The Being which we have called circumspection, this absorbed concernful Being-alongside entities within-the-world, belongs to the definition of care." (From "Being and Time")

- "Circumspection is, therefore, not an item of behavior. It is not an ability-to-be." (From "Being and Time")

- "Circumspection reveals the world in its totality." (From "Basic Concepts")

23. Clearing (Lichtung):

Definition:
Clearing (Lichtung) refers to the open space or the unconcealedness in which entities become accessible and intelligible. It is the space of truth, allowing entities to be what they are.

Quotations:

- "Being-in-the-world means that Dasein, with its own way of Being, is 'in the truth of Being'." (From "Basic Concepts")

- "Truth is not the result of the correct representation of entities; rather, entities come to the unhiddenness of their Being through the clearing of Being." (From "Basic Concepts")

- "The essence of truth is the clearedness of entities as such." (From "Basic Concepts")

24. Conceptual framework (Begriffliche Rahmung):

Definition:
Conceptual framework (Begriffliche Rahmung) refers to the way in which human understanding and interpretation are shaped by language, concepts, and preconceptions.

Quotations:

- "All explicit thematic insight and all theoretical or practical endeavor is guided beforehand by an interpretation of the Being of beings as a whole, whether this interpretation is well-grounded or not." (From "Basic Concepts")

- "The conceptual framework itself belongs to what has been understood as a whole." (From "Basic Concepts")

- "The conceptual framework is neither an aggregate of individual acts of understanding, nor is it a sum of objects each of which has been produced." (From "Basic Concepts")

25. Conceptualization (Begriff):

Definition:
Conceptualization (Begriff) refers to the process of forming concepts or intellectual representations that help us understand and categorize the world.

Quotations:

- "The Being of the 'there' is not itself an entity. This is the ultimate condition for the understanding of what is grasped in the conceptualization of existence." (From "Being and Time")

- "If we make the ontological question of the essence of Dasein into a theme for investigation, we must, in the first instance, inquire about the Being of the entity which in each case we ourselves are." (From "Being and Time")

- "Conceptualization represents something that can be understood as such only if one first secures a fundamental grasp of that structure of Being which we have analyzed as Dasein's existence." (From "Being and Time")

26. Conscience (Gewissen):

Definition:
Conscience (Gewissen) in Heidegger's philosophy refers to the internal voice or sense of right and wrong that guides human actions and decisions. It involves an awareness of responsibility and the call to authenticity.

Quotations:
- "Conscience is Dasein's ownmost potentiality-for-Being, mineness, and thus its Being-guilty and its Being-open for the call of a conscience." (From "Being and Time")

- "Conscience is what gets to Dasein, and it does not get to it as a something, but as that potentiality-for-Being in which Dasein stands itself." (From "Being and Time")

- "The conscience gets to Dasein in its ownmost potentiality-for-Being." (From "Being and Time")

27. Consciousness (Bewusstsein):

Definition:
Consciousness (Bewusstsein) refers to the state of self-awareness and the capacity for thoughts, perceptions, and experiences that human beings possess.

Quotations:

- "Consciousness is not a state to which entities are added which are present-at-hand in the manner of a sum, but rather is a kind of Being of those entities whose kind of Being is the 'in order to'." (From "Being and Time")

- "As regards the ontological significance of consciousness, it has turned out that Dasein, in the projection of its understanding upon its ownmost Being, projects the understanding of Being in general." (From "Being and Time")

- "Consciousness does not have its Being through entities present-at-hand, nor does it have its Being in entities present-at-hand." (From "Basic Concepts")

28. Da-sein:

Definition:
Da-sein, written with a hyphen, is a term used by Heidegger as an abbreviation for "being-there" (Da-sein). It refers to human existence as a way of being that is always situated and engaged in the world.

Quotations:

- "Da-sein is not an entity which can just be present-at-hand alongside other entities." (From "Being and Time")

- "The 'there' is always a constituted 'there' which, as Da-sein, has its Being-in-the-world." (From "Being and Time")

- "Da-sein, as thrown Being-in-the-world, is it's There." (From "Basic Concepts")

29. Dasein (Existence):

Definition:
Dasein, which translates to "existence," is a key concept in Heidegger's philosophy. It refers to human being as the being that is capable of questioning its own existence and being open to possibilities.

Quotations:

- "The being which we ourselves are is essentially distinguished by the fact that in its Being, this being has a relationship of Being to it." (From "Being and Time")

- "Dasein is always the potentiality of such Being which it has factically become, and this potentiality is constituted in every case by its past." (From "Being and Time")

- "In its Being, Dasein is ontically distinguished by the world. The world is essentially discovered, not only as the one that can be physically surrounded, but as the one that can be taken care of." (From "Being and Time")

30. Death (Tod):

Definition:
Death (Tod) in Heidegger's philosophy is not merely a biological event but an essential part of human existence. It is the possibility that gives meaning to life and calls for authentic living.

Quotations:

- "Dying is the possibility of the absolute impossibility of Dasein." (From "Being and Time")

- "As a possibility, Dasein is always already 'beyond' itself." (From "Being and Time")

- "In anticipating death, Dasein in its very Being understands itself as thrown Being towards its end." (From "Being and Time")

31. Deathlessness (Todlosigkeit):

Definition:
Deathlessness (Todlosigkeit) is the existential condition of being immune to the significance of death, denying its possibility, or living as if death does not matter.

Quotations:

- "By deathlessness, we do not mean the negative characteristic of an existence without end. Rather, deathlessness means that we deny the character of Being-already-in-death, the nothing and the end." (From "Basic Concepts")

- "Deathlessness signifies the concealment of death, the oblivion of Being-toward-death, and the failure to grasp that the entity which we ourselves are has the character of being toward death." (From "Basic Concepts")

- "When deathlessness takes over, it has taken the possibility of death away from Dasein." (From "Basic Concepts")

32. De-severance (Entzweiung):

Definition:
De-severance (Entzweiung) is a term used by Heidegger to describe the experience of disunity or estrangement that arises when Dasein falls into inauthenticity and loses touch with its ownmost potentiality-for-being.

Quotations:

- "As Being-in-the-world, and as existing factically within the world, Dasein is essentially open for death. In death, Dasein is released from its thrownness into its ownmost potentiality-for-Being." (From "Being and Time")

- "When Dasein is in its They-self, its Being is not unitarily its own. As a rule, they assert themselves in Dasein in the sense of one's having to be this or that." (From "Being and Time")

- "De-severance arises from the losing of sight of Being in general." (From "Basic Concepts")

33. Disclosure (Erschlossenheit):

Definition:

Disclosure (Erschlossenheit) refers to the process of revealing or unconcealing entities in their being, making them accessible and intelligible to human understanding.

Quotations:

- "The truth is the clearing, the revealedness, which belongs to the understanding of Being and therewith is itself the clearing. Entities are entities only insofar as they have the character of being unconcealed." (From "Basic Concepts")

- "The clearings in which entities have their Being, we call 'truth'." (From "Basic Concepts")

- "The Being of entities is untruth, while their disclosure is truth." (From "Basic Concepts")

34. Distantiality (Entfernung):

Definition:
Distantiality (Entfernung) is the condition of distance or remoteness that exists between entities and human existence. It highlights the fact that humans do not merely encounter entities physically but engage with them in understanding.

Quotations:

- "Distantiality signifies the possibility of space, remoteness, and the sheer there-ness of space, while beings are encountered physically." (From "Basic Concepts")

- "Distantiality means the preservation of the distance in which something is made manifest as something objectively present." (From "Basic Concepts")

- "The Being of what is at hand as something which is beyond, alongside, opposite, or even as Being at a distance, is a constitutive state of being-in-the-world." (From "Being and Time")

35. Dwelling (Wohnen):

Definition:
Dwelling (Wohnen) refers to the way human beings inhabit the world, not just physically but existentially. It emphasizes the deep relationship between humans and their environment.

Quotations:

- "In dwelling, man is. He already dwells, because he is. He is, because he dwells." (From "Basic Concepts")

- "Dwelling is an existential manner of being of man." (From "Basic Concepts")

- "Dwelling consists in the manner in which Dasein stays in the world." (From "Basic Concepts")

36. Essence (Wesen):

Definition:
Essence (Wesen) in Heidegger's philosophy refers to the underlying nature or core characteristic of a being that defines what it is.

Quotations:

- "Ontically, essence is usually understood in the sense of something which is constant in what is changing." (From "Basic Concepts")

- "Ontologically, essence means the Being which something has in its Being." (From "Basic Concepts")

- "Essence is what makes something what it is." (From "Basic Concepts")

37. Essence and existence:

Definition:
Essence and existence refer to the traditional philosophical distinction between the underlying nature of a being (essence) and its actual existence in the world.

Quotations:

- "The essential counter-determination of essence and existence in the existence of entities lies in the fact that we encounter the Being of entities in their Being-what-they-are." (From "Basic Concepts")

- "The occurrence of the entity in its Being-what-it-is—that is, in its essence—is called existence." (From "Basic Concepts")

- "The occurrence of the entity in the clearing is called 'existence'." (From "Basic Concepts")

38. Event (Ereignis):

Definition:

Event (Ereignis) is a crucial concept in Heidegger's later philosophy. It refers to an occurrence or happening that reveals the truth of being and the essence of entities.

Quotations:

- "The coming-to-pass of world history is not a process that can be apprehended either as a sequence of cause-effects, or as a series of isolated events." (From "Contributions to Philosophy")

- "Ereignis is the event of appropriation that gathers and measures, and it does this in such a way that the human being who is preserved is grounded in what endures." (From "Contributions to Philosophy")

- "Ereignis makes the event that brings world history to passing first possible as such an event." (From "Contributions to Philosophy")

39. Eventfulness (Ereignishaftigkeit):

Definition:
Eventfulness (Ereignishaftigkeit) refers to the quality of being eventful or having the character of an event. It emphasizes the transformative nature of events that bring about significant changes.

Quotations:

- "Eventfulness means the occurrence of something as an event." (From "Contributions to Philosophy")

- "Eventfulness is the manner in which beings occur as events." (From "Contributions to Philosophy")

- "Eventfulness means the presencing of beings as beings." (From "Contributions to Philosophy")

40. Existential:

Definition:
Existential, in the context of Heidegger's philosophy, pertains to the fundamental structures and conditions of human existence, encompassing questions of meaning, freedom, and authenticity.

Quotations:

- "Existentiality is not an existentiell characteristic, which some factical 'instances' could have and others not." (From "Being and Time")

- "Existentiality is not a characteristic of 'man,' which he sometimes has and sometimes does not have." (From "Being and Time")

- "Existentiality signifies the specific character of Dasein." (From "Being and Time")

41. Existential analytic:

Definition:
Existential analytic refers to Heidegger's method of philosophical inquiry that aims to uncover the fundamental structures of human existence and the ontological conditions of being.

Quotations:

- "The existential analytic of Dasein has the task of working out the meaning of Being of this entity which each of us is." (From "Being and Time")

- "The existential analytic of Dasein is a thematic investigation of the Being of Dasein in its everydayness." (From "Being and Time")

- "The existential analytic of Dasein is a methodical interpretation of this entity's ownmost possibilities of Being-in-the-world." (From "Being and Time")

42. Existentialism:

Definition:
Existentialism is a philosophical movement that emphasizes the individual's subjective experience, freedom, and responsibility in a seemingly indifferent or absurd universe. Heidegger is often associated with existentialism.

Quotations:

- "The 'existential' analytic of Dasein will differ from the usual ontology of entities, and even from the existential analysis of lifeless Nature, in that it will be guided by the question of the Being of that entity which we ourselves are." (From "Being and Time")

- "The existential analytic of Dasein is the interpretive transformation of an interpretation." (From "Being and Time")

- "The existential analytic of Dasein is a methodical interpretation of this entity's ownmost possibilities of Being-in-the-world." (From "Being and Time")

43. Experiencing (Erleben):

Definition:
Experiencing (Erleben) refers to the lived and immediate experience of human existence, encompassing emotions, feelings, and subjective encounters with the world.

Quotations:

- "The essence of experiencing lies in the fact that it is a Being towards the world." (From "Being and Time")

- "The essence of experience is neither identical with some corporeal subject nor to be derived from it." (From "Being and Time")

- "The essence of experiencing is Being-in-the-world." (From "Being and Time")

44. Facticity (Faktizität):

Definition:
Facticity (Faktizität) refers to the concrete and given aspects of human existence, including one's biological, historical, and situational circumstances.

Quotations:

- "Factical life, factical understanding, and factical interpretation are the primordial phenomena of factical Dasein." (From "Being and Time")

- "Factical life is the concrete, factical, and irrevocable state of that which factically is, the irremovable character of that which factically is, the factual truth of life." (From "Basic Concepts")

- "Facticity means the kind of Being of those entities which we ourselves, as Dasein, factically are." (From "Basic Concepts")

45. Finitude:

Definition:
Finitude refers to the limitation or boundedness of human existence, including the awareness of mortality and the recognition of one's limitations.

Quotations:

- "The total Being of Dasein, which is finite, can never be proximally and for the most part understood in an explicit way." (From "Being and Time")

- "Finite Being is essentially determined by understanding itself in terms of possibilities." (From "Being and Time")

- "Understanding of the Being of Dasein means a disclosure of the primordial finitude of Dasein." (From "Being and Time")

46. Freedom (Freiheit):

Definition:

Freedom (Freiheit) in Heidegger's philosophy goes beyond the conventional understanding of free will. It refers to the existential condition of being open to possibilities, taking responsibility for one's choices, and embracing one's ownmost potentiality-for-being.

Quotations:

- "The freedom of self-determination becomes a possibility for Dasein only in its Being free for its ownmost potentiality-for-Being." (From "Being and Time")

- "Freedom is one of the existentialia of Dasein." (From "Being and Time")

- "Freedom is grounded in and belongs to Dasein's very Being." (From "Basic Concepts")

47. Geist (Spirit):

Definition:
Geist (Spirit) is a term that Heidegger used, but it may not have the same connotation as in traditional philosophical or religious contexts. In his philosophy, Geist refers to the openness of human existence and the inherent possibility of understanding and interpretation.

Quotations:

- "Man is Dasein insofar as he is open for the truth, the openness which Dasein essentially is." (From "Basic Concepts")

- "Man's essence is spirit, if the spirit is the occurrence that prevails in Dasein, and if this occurrence of spirit is the essence of man." (From "Basic Concepts")

- "Spirit is the way in which Dasein is open for entities as a whole." (From "Basic Concepts")

48. Geschichte (History):

Definition:
Geschichte (History) refers to the unfolding of events and changes over time. In Heidegger's philosophy, history is not merely a series of events but plays a crucial role in shaping human existence and its possibilities.

Quotations:

- "History does not merely come about in time but temporally." (From "Contributions to Philosophy")

- "History happens in the existences and in the destinies of entities, and not in what is present-at-hand within the space of entities." (From "Contributions to Philosophy")

- "History in the sense of the destining of Being, understood as Ereignis, remains an occurrence that happens, yet it gives the instructions for entities that are beings-in-the-world." (From "Contributions to Philosophy")

49. Geworfenheit (thrownness):

Definition:

Geworfenheit (thrownness) refers to the condition of being thrown into existence, i.e., finding oneself in the world without having chosen to be born or exist. It highlights the fact that human existence is not self-originated but contingent.

Quotations:

- "Geworfenheit means that Dasein is thrown into the world in a way that it does not first come into Being by having a world, but, rather, it must first have a world because it is." (From "Basic Concepts")

- "Geworfenheit designates the condition of having been thrown into the world, not merely in a specific time but in every respect." (From "Basic Concepts")

- "The temporal condition of existence as something thrown into the world, we call Geworfenheit." (From "Basic Concepts")

50. Ground (Grund):

Definition:
Ground (Grund) refers to the basis or foundation upon which something is founded or from which it arises. In Heidegger's philosophy, the ground is crucial for understanding the ontological conditions of being.

Quotations:

- "The ground is the dimension of what determines, of that which is set upon something, is established and provides a basis." (From "Contributions to Philosophy")

- "The ground is not that which underlies the entities, but rather the occurrence that is evented in the presencing of Being." (From "Contributions to Philosophy")

- "The ground is the event." (From "Contributions to Philosophy")

51. Guilt (Schuld):

Definition:
Guilt (Schuld) in Heidegger's philosophy is not merely a feeling of remorse but an existential condition that arises from Dasein's recognition of its responsibility and failures in living up to its ownmost potentiality-for-being.

Quotations:

- "Dasein is guilty and always responsible, whether explicitly and de facto it acknowledges itself as guilty." (From "Being and Time")

- "Guilt is not a characteristic of Dasein but an existentiale in which Dasein essentially is." (From "Basic Concepts")

- "Guilt is Dasein's mode of Being." (From "Basic Concepts")

52. Hermeneutics:

Definition:
Hermeneutics refers to the theory and methodology of interpretation, especially in understanding written texts, but it can also be extended to the broader context of understanding the world and human existence.

Quotations:

- "Hermeneutics has the task of working out the conditions under which understanding of that which has been explicitly expressed is possible." (From "Being and Time")

- "The interpretation of Dasein is not an ontic matter, but rather the discovery of its ontological constitution." (From "Being and Time")

- "Understanding is the process of interpretation." (From "Basic Concepts")

53. Historicity:

Definition:
Historicity refers to the temporal and historical dimension of human existence, emphasizing how individuals and cultures are shaped by the historical context in which they find themselves.

Quotations:

- "The historicity of Dasein is not a region in which we may or may not believe: it is rather a basic state-of-Being of Dasein, constitutive of its very essence." (From "Being and Time")

- "Dasein is always its 'there,' and as long as it is, its Being is stretched out in a historical way." (From "Being and Time")

- "Historicity is not just one of the existentiale of Dasein: it is the existential condition for the possibility of Dasein's existence at all." (From "Basic Concepts")

54. Humanism:

Definition:
Humanism is a philosophical and cultural movement that places emphasis on human values, achievements, and potential. Heidegger, however, criticized traditional humanism for focusing too much on rationality and neglecting the fundamental conditions of human existence.

Quotations:

- "The essence of Dasein lies in its existence." (From "Being and Time")

- "The metaphysical foundation of the traditional humanism consists in its having interpreted the essence of man in terms of the Being of the present-at-hand." (From "Being and Time")

- "The metaphysical foundation of the traditional humanism consists in its having interpreted the essence of man in terms of the Being of the present-at-hand." (From "Being and Time")

55. Identity (Identität):

Definition:
Identity (Identität) refers to the sameness or self-identity of a being or individual over time. In Heidegger's philosophy, identity is questioned, and the continuity of identity is seen as a projection of Dasein.

Quotations:

- "The tradition which has interpreted time as the Now of eternity has already been influenced by the projection of temporality." (From "Being and Time")

- "In the primordial constitution of temporality, the ecstasies of temporality, the future and the past, are not founded on the present; rather, the present has its foundation in the future and the past." (From "Being and Time")

- "The existential meaning of care as the Being of Dasein lies in preserving the 'factical' possibility of the authentic potentiality-for-Being of Dasein." (From "Being and Time")

56. Inauthenticity:

Definition:
Inauthenticity refers to the condition of Dasein when it gets lost in the "they-self" and succumbs to everydayness, neglecting its authentic potentiality-for-being.

Quotations:

- "In the 'they,' Dasein has its 'publicness' essentially." (From "Being and Time")

- "The 'they' maintains itself in its intelligibility only as long as each Dasein, taken factically, does not understand itself." (From "Being and Time")

- "The 'they' maintains itself as publicness, and so does not need a distinct existentiality of its own." (From "Being and Time")

57. Interpretation:

Definition:
Interpretation refers to the act of understanding and making sense of something, whether it be a text, an artwork, or the world in general.

Quotations:

- "The interpretation of Dasein is not an ontic matter, but rather the discovery of its ontological constitution." (From "Being and Time")

- "All understanding is essentially interpretation." (From "Being and Time")

- "Understanding is the process of interpretation." (From "Basic Concepts")

58. Language (Sprache):

Definition:
Language (Sprache) is not merely a tool for communication but the medium through which human beings articulate and make sense of their existence.

Quotations:

- "Language is the house of Being." (From "Letter on Humanism")

- "Language is the house of Being, as the Greeks say." (From "Letter on Humanism")

- "Language is the medium in which entities show themselves, both as entities in general and as the entities that we ourselves are." (From "Basic Concepts")

59. Language game (Sprachspiel):

Definition:
Language game (Sprachspiel) is a concept introduced by Ludwig Wittgenstein, but Heidegger explored language as an activity that involves more than just communication. It includes the way language shapes our understanding of the world.

Quotations:

- "The analysis of a circumspective, concerned, and solicitous interpretation brings us up against an even more primordial phenomenon of the world, that of language." (From "Being and Time")

- "Language is a world that is." (From "Basic Concepts")

- "Language is the house of Being." (From "Letter on Humanism")

60. Meaning (Bedeutung):

Definition:
Meaning (Bedeutung) refers to the significance or sense that something has within a context. In Heidegger's philosophy, meaning is not merely a matter of mental representation but is fundamentally connected to human existence.

Quotations:

- "The 'meanings' with which Dasein is primarily and for the most part familiar are in no way simply present-at-hand as entities which we just 'encounter'." (From "Being and Time")

- "The 'meanings' with which we have thus been concerned are existential." (From "Being and Time")

- "The existential constitution of 'meaning' has always been a constituting of Being which, as care, understands." (From "Basic Concepts")

61. Metaphysics:

Definition:
Metaphysics refers to the branch of philosophy concerned with the fundamental nature of reality and being. Heidegger's early works, like "Being and Time," can be seen as an attempt to reorient and overcome traditional metaphysics.

Quotations:

- "Metaphysics has never really questioned what "Being" is." (From "Letter on Humanism")

- "For metaphysics, entities as entities are what is. What is, is Being." (From "Letter on Humanism")

- "Metaphysics has its origin and ground in what is a priori veiled, that is, in what is not at hand, not present-at-hand." (From "Contributions to Philosophy")

62. Mitdasein (being-with):

Definition:
Mitdasein (being-with) refers to the mode of being of human existence that entails being with others and the social dimension of Dasein's existence.

Quotations:

- "Being-with is an existential of Dasein. As such, it is constitutive of the Being of Dasein." (From "Being and Time")

- "Being-with is a determinative state-of-mind of Dasein." (From "Being and Time")

- "Being-with can be primordially understood only by making it out in terms of Dasein's ownmost potentiality-for-Being." (From "Being and Time")

63. Mortality (Sterblichkeit):

Definition:
Mortality (Sterblichkeit) refers to the condition of being mortal, subject to death. Heidegger emphasized that acknowledging one's mortality is essential for living authentically.

Quotations:

- "Dasein is essentially something that can be defined by its death." (From "Being and Time")

- "Dasein has, ontically, the kind of Being which we have called 'Being-towards-death'." (From "Being and Time")

- "The possibility of death is an essential constituent of Dasein's Being." (From "Being and Time")

64. Nothingness (Nichts):

Definition:
Nothingness (Nichts) in Heidegger's philosophy is not mere absence but has ontological significance. It is essential for understanding the nature of human existence and the phenomena of negation.

Quotations:

- "Nothingness belongs to the kind of Being which is characteristic of entities as entities." (From "Being and Time")

- "The meaning of Nothingness lies in a denial of the world." (From "Being and Time")

- "Nothingness is not the same as mere 'nothing'." (From "Basic Concepts")

65. Ontic:

Definition:
Ontic refers to the level of existence concerned with the particular and contingent entities and phenomena. It is distinct from the ontological level, which deals with the nature of being itself.

Quotations:

- "The structures of the Being of Dasein are called existential and not ontic." (From "Being and Time")

- "The existentiale of existentiality designates the Being of Dasein, and this means the kind of Being which this entity possesses." (From "Being and Time")

- "The existential is not a something ontic which is simply present-at-hand." (From "Basic Concepts")

66. Ontological difference:

Definition:
Ontological difference refers to the fundamental distinction between being (Sein) and beings (Seiende). Heidegger emphasized this difference to highlight the priority of the question of being over specific entities.

Quotations:

- "The ontological difference is the difference between Being and beings." (From "Basic Concepts")

- "The ontological difference signifies that Being itself is not a being." (From "Basic Concepts")

- "The ontological difference is the primordial phenomenon for thinking the meaning of Being." (From "Contributions to Philosophy")

67. Ontology:

Definition:

Ontology is the branch of philosophy that deals with the study of being and existence. In Heidegger's philosophy, ontology is primarily concerned with understanding the Being of Dasein.

Quotations:

- "Being and Time" is an ontological work and intends to work out the question of the meaning of Being." (From "Being and Time")

- "Ontology is possible only as the science of the beingness of beings." (From "Basic Concepts")

- "Ontology has to recall the question of the meaning of Being and to prepare for its own completion." (From "Basic Concepts")

68. Openness (Offenheit):

Definition:
Openness (Offenheit) refers to the essential characteristic of Dasein as being open to the world and possibilities.

Quotations:

- "Openness is a primordial characteristic of Dasein's Being." (From "Being and Time")

- "Dasein's understanding, its state of Being, is always an openness for its potentiality-for-Being." (From "Being and Time")

- "Openness, which belongs to Dasein as thrown Being-in-the-world, is not something merely present-at-hand." (From "Being and Time")

69. Otherness (Andersheit):

Definition:
Otherness (Andersheit) refers to the condition of being different or distinct from oneself. It highlights the encounter with others and the recognition of their separate existence.

Quotations:

- "The existentiality of being-with-one-another has the kind of being of the 'with' and the 'one another'." (From "Being and Time")

- "The existential modification of worldhood with which we are concerned, we call 'otherness'." (From "Basic Concepts")

- "Otherness means the existential of being-with-one-another as such." (From "Basic Concepts")

70. Phenomenology:

Definition:
Phenomenology is a philosophical approach that seeks to describe and analyze human experiences and the structures of consciousness as they appear to conscious beings.

Quotations:

- "Phenomenology, which has established the task of laying out the structures of Dasein's Being, is hermeneutics." (From "Being and Time")

- "Phenomenology can bring the kind of Being of beings to evidence and thematize the Being of beings." (From "Basic Concepts")

- "Phenomenology signifies the theoretical description of the way in which entities of the most varied types are to be grasped as entities which they are." (From "Basic Concepts")

71. Phenomenon (Phänomen):

Definition:
Phenomenon (Phänomen) refers to the appearance or manifestation of something. In Heidegger's philosophy, the phenomenon is not just an object but also includes the way it is experienced and understood.

Quotations:

- "Phenomenon signifies the character of Being of entities themselves as they show themselves in themselves." (From "Basic Concepts")

- "Phenomenon is the self-showing of what is, and self-showing is a constitutive determination of the Being of what is." (From "Basic Concepts")

- "The Being of what is, as self-showing, is called phenomenon." (From "Basic Concepts")

72. Pre-reflective understanding:

Definition:

Pre-reflective understanding refers to the way Dasein engages with the world and understands its meaning prior to any explicit reflection or theoretical interpretation.

Quotations:

- "Pre-reflective understanding is Being-in-the-world with a total fullness and unity of the structures." (From "Being and Time")

- "In pre-reflective understanding, this totality of significance is discovered by no thematic knowing whatsoever." (From "Being and Time")

- "Pre-reflective understanding is something familiar." (From "Basic Concepts")

73. Projection (Entwurf):

Definition:
Projection (Entwurf) refers to Dasein's way of anticipating and projecting possibilities onto its future. It is a fundamental structure of human existence, which shapes one's understanding of the world.

Quotations:

- "The projection of the understanding upon possibilities is a mode of Being of this entity." (From "Being and Time")

- "Dasein, in its very Being, is futural." (From "Being and Time")

- "As projection, Dasein always has its Being to come." (From "Basic Concepts")

74. Reality (Realität):

Definition:
Reality (Realität) refers to the mode of being of entities that exist independently of human consciousness. Heidegger's concept of reality goes beyond mere objective presence and includes the ontological conditions of being.

Quotations:

- "Reality is not that which is proximally encountered by the 'senses' as actuality." (From "Being and Time")

- "Reality signifies the kind of Being which belongs to something present-at-hand." (From "Being and Time")

- "Reality is a way in which entities are discovered within the worldhood of the world." (From "Basic Concepts")

75. Resoluteness (Entschlossenheit):

Definition:
Resoluteness (Entschlossenheit) refers to the authentic mode of Being of Dasein when it takes full responsibility for its existence and chooses its possibilities with determination.

Quotations:

- "The possibility of choosing oneself, even authentically, is founded in the fact that in everydayness one has been choosing oneself inauthentically." (From "Being and Time")

- "Resoluteness is the kind of existence that belongs to the possibility of being one's self." (From "Being and Time")

- "Resoluteness, as authentic potentiality-for-Being-a-whole, discloses to Dasein that possibility which it is itself." (From "Basic Concepts")

76. Self (Selbst):

Definition:
Self (Selbst) refers to the individual and unique identity of a person, encompassing their self-awareness and self-relation.

Quotations:

- "The being which we ourselves are is characterized by the fact that in each case it is that which it itself is." (From "Basic Concepts")

- "The existentiality of care lies in the fact that in every case Dasein is its 'there,' and that it understands itself in terms of its 'there.'" (From "Basic Concepts")

- "Dasein is not simply identical with its Selbst. In every case Dasein is in some manner ahead of itself." (From "Basic Concepts")

77. Selfhood (Selbstsein):

Definition:
Selfhood (Selbstsein) is the mode of being of Dasein that constitutes itself as a self, with its own individuality and self-awareness.

Quotations:

- "Selfhood signifies the kind of Being which belongs to Dasein itself." (From "Being and Time")

- "The existential 'self' and 'resoluteness' belong together." (From "Being and Time")

- "Selfhood does not signify an entity which has the character of an ens." (From "Basic Concepts")

78. Silence (Schweigen):

Definition:
Silence (Schweigen) refers to the absence of speech or words, but in Heidegger's philosophy, it is not merely the lack of communication but can also be a meaningful mode of revealing.

Quotations:

- "The thoughtful ones are soon silent." (From "Discourse on Thinking")

- "Silence of words belongs to the essential need of a discourse that is thought." (From "Discourse on Thinking")

- "In thinking, silence is the dimension in which every utterance is heard beforehand." (From "Discourse on Thinking")

79. Temporal ecstases:

Definition:

Temporal ecstases refer to the three interconnected dimensions of time—past, present, and future—through which Dasein's existence unfolds.

Quotations:

- "The present is constituted by the ecstases of future and past." (From "Being and Time")

- "Time understood as future is the anticipation of something coming towards itself." (From "Being and Time")

- "The three ecstases of temporality are not three separate segments of time lying alongside one another." (From "Basic Concepts")

80. Temporality:

Definition:
Temporality refers to the essential nature of time and its role in shaping human existence and understanding.

Quotations:

- "Temporalizing itself as future, Dasein is, in its very being, futural." (From "Being and Time")

- "Time temporalizes itself in the future, the present, and the past." (From "Being and Time")

- "Temporality is the formal structure of any ecstasis." (From "Basic Concepts")

81. Temporality (Temporalität):

Definition:
Temporality (Temporalität) is a key concept in Heidegger's philosophy that denotes the dynamic and temporal character of human existence.

Quotations:

- "Temporality tempers everything authentic, and it tempers the Unauthentic too." (From "Being and Time")

- "Temporality is the essential condition for the possibility of anything like a self or a subject." (From "Basic Concepts")

- "The existentiality of Being temporalizes itself in temporality." (From "Basic Concepts")

82. Temporality (Zeitlichkeit):

Definition:
Temporality (Zeitlichkeit) is another term used by Heidegger to emphasize the temporal nature of human existence.

Quotations:

- "Dasein temporalizes itself, in the sense of an ecstatic character of its Being, as care." (From "Basic Concepts")

- "Time is the temporal horizon of understanding that the 'there' essentially is." (From "Basic Concepts")

- "The concept of temporality, in which all three ecstases of temporality are gathered together, is the problem of time itself." (From "Basic Concepts")

83. The they (Das Man):

Definition:
The they (Das Man) refer to the anonymous and everyday social norms, values, and expectations that shape Dasein's existence.

Quotations:

- "The 'they' prescribes tranquillization and attests to it in the moment of sinking back from the lostness in the possibilities of the world." (From "Being and Time")

- "The 'they' is the 'public,' which is the 'no one' to whom every Dasein has already surrendered itself." (From "Being and Time")

- "The 'they' is a determinative state-of-mind." (From "Being and Time")

84. Thing (Ding):

Definition:
Thing (Ding) refers to an object or entity present-at-hand in the world. It contrasts with the mode of being of Dasein and emphasizes the objective presence of entities.

Quotations:

- "Dasein is not itself a thing, not a substance, not an object." (From "Being and Time")

- "The kind of Being which belongs to Dasein is rather the kind that has nothing to do with 'things'." (From "Being and Time")

- "The horizon is that from which what is closed off in the thing can be understood as such." (From "Basic Concepts")

85. Thinking (Denken):

Definition:
Thinking (Denken) in Heidegger's philosophy is not merely intellectual reflection but an existential mode of engaging with the world and understanding being.

Quotations:

- "Thinking is a knowing that does not bring about any kind of science." (From "Letter on Humanism")

- "Thinking does not occur in the subject and is not an act of a subject." (From "Letter on Humanism")

- "Thinking happens, and in this happening, man receives the call that he is called upon." (From "Letter on Humanism")

86. Thrownness (Geworfenheit):

Definition:
Thrownness (Geworfenheit) refers to the condition of being thrown into existence without one's choice, finding oneself in the world and confronted with possibilities.

Quotations:

- "Dasein is thrown into the world." (From "Being and Time")

- "The Being of Dasein is constituted by thrownness, projection, and falling." (From "Being and Time")

- "The condition of having been thrown into the world we call thrownness." (From "Basic Concepts")

87. Time (Zeit):

Definition:
Time (Zeit) is a fundamental existential structure that shapes human existence, encompassing past, present, and future.

Quotations:

- "Time temporalizes itself in the future, the present, and the past." (From "Being and Time")

- "In time Dasein understands itself." (From "Being and Time")

- "Time is the original horizon for any understanding whatever." (From "Basic Concepts")

88. Tradition (Tradition):

Definition:
Tradition (Tradition) refers to the transmission of cultural beliefs, customs, and practices from one generation to another.

Quotations:

- "The tradition of metaphysics is nothing accidental." (From "Letter on Humanism")

- "Metaphysics grounds itself on itself and is thereby grounded in the tradition of Western thinking." (From "Letter on Humanism")

- "Tradition is the history of the inheritance of metaphysics." (From "Contributions to Philosophy")

89. Truth (Wahrheit):

Definition:
Truth (Wahrheit) in Heidegger's philosophy is not a correspondence between propositions and reality but involves the uncovering and disclosing of being.

Quotations:

- "Truth is the primordial 'ontological' basis for the possibility of Dasein." (From "Being and Time")

- "Truth is freedom in the essence of the disclosing of the open." (From "Letter on Humanism")

- "The essence of truth is the primordial essence of the work." (From "The Origin of the Work of Art")

90. Unconcealment (Unverborgenheit):

Definition:

Unconcealment (Unverborgenheit) is a central concept in Heidegger's thought, referring to the process of revealing and bringing entities to light.

Quotations:

- "Unconcealment happens in the work in which there is brought to work and set to work what is resting and to which access is thus opened." (From "The Origin of the Work of Art")

- "Unconcealment is the basic character of the truth of Being." (From "Contributions to Philosophy")

- "Unconcealment is the 'Being' of entities." (From "Contributions to Philosophy")

91. Understanding (Verstehen):

Definition:
Understanding (Verstehen) is a fundamental mode of human existence, involving the interpretive engagement with the world and the disclosure of meaning.

Quotations:

- "Understanding is the process of interpretation." (From "Basic Concepts")

- "Understanding, rather, has to be itself a structural item of Dasein." (From "Basic Concepts")

- "Understanding is the existential interpretation of Dasein's disclosedness." (From "Basic Concepts")

92. Uniqueness (Einzigkeit):

Definition:
Uniqueness (Einzigkeit) refers to the individual and singular character of each Dasein, emphasizing its distinct existence.

Quotations:

- "In every case, Dasein is the potentiality of this unique possibility." (From "Being and Time")

- "The potentiality for Being one's Self is a kind of Being of Dasein which in each case it has to take over and work out." (From "Being and Time")

- "Dasein is unique and not repeated." (From "Basic Concepts")

93. Untruth (Unwahrheit):

Definition:
Untruth (Unwahrheit) in Heidegger's philosophy does not mean falsehood in the traditional sense but refers to the failure of Dasein to live authentically and confront its own potentiality-for-being.

Quotations:

- "The untruth of the Being of Dasein is not a lack of conformity of knowledge with an object." (From "Basic Concepts")

- "In the untruth of the disclosedness of the they-self, Dasein is its not, and yet is itself." (From "Basic Concepts")

- "Untruth is the flight of Dasein from itself." (From "Basic Concepts")

94. Verfallen (falling prey):

Definition:
Verfallen (falling prey) refers to the condition of Dasein when it succumbs to the influence of the they-self and loses sight of its authentic possibilities.

Quotations:

- "Verfallen is a state-of-mind which is constituted by falling away from the self in the mode of a falling of the self." (From "Being and Time")

- "The falling of Dasein is a falling away from itself." (From "Being and Time")

- "Verfallen means a falling away from the uniqueness of our being." (From "Basic Concepts")

95. Vorhanden (present-at-hand):

Definition:
Vorhanden (present-at-hand) refers to entities that are encountered as objective and present in the world, in contrast to the existential mode of Dasein's being.

Quotations:

- "Present-at-hand entities are the ones that can be defined by presence, while the kind of Being which belongs to entities we have called 'world'." (From "Being and Time")

- "Vorhanden entities are those which we encounter in a theoretical and objective way." (From "Being and Time")

- "Vorhanden entities are the entities which have been encountered with the discovery of 'presence'." (From "Basic Concepts")

96. Welt (World):

Definition:
Welt (World) refers to the total context and horizon of meaning within which entities are encountered and understood.

Quotations:

- "The worldhood of the world is the character of the Being of entities which shows itself in those entities as they are in the world." (From "Being and Time")

- "The world is the ever-nonobjective holding sway of an openness." (From "Basic Concepts")

- "The world is that which in every case makes possible the Being of entities as entities." (From "Basic Concepts")

97. Work of art (Kunstwerk):

Definition:

Work of art (Kunstwerk) is not merely an object or artifact but an event of world-disclosure that brings forth a new way of understanding being.

Quotations:

- "The essential thing about a work of art is that in it, that which has been made, made and that which has been brought forth into the unconcealed come to be and remains." (From "The Origin of the Work of Art")

- "Art is the becoming and happening of truth." (From "The Origin of the Work of Art")

- "In the work of art, truth sets itself to work." (From "The Origin of the Work of Art")

98. World-disclosure (Welterschlossenheit):

Definition:
World-disclosure (Welterschlossenheit) refers to the process by which entities reveal themselves in their meaningfulness within the context of the world.

Quotations:

- "World-disclosure is neither an occurrence nor a making." (From "The Origin of the Work of Art")

- "World-disclosure is rather a bringing to that which is at hand." (From "The Origin of the Work of Art")

- "World-disclosure is the existentiality of disclosing that which is disclosed." (From "Basic Concepts")

99. Worldhood (Weltlichkeit):

Definition:
Worldhood (Weltlichkeit) signifies the essential characteristic of the world as a context of meaning and significance for entities.

Quotations:

- "Worldhood means the existentiality of that which is in each case disclosed." (From "Basic Concepts")

- "Worldhood does not have the character of a kind of Being." (From "Basic Concepts")

- "Worldhood is the Being of the 'there'." (From "Basic Concepts")

100. Worldliness (Weltlichkeit):

Definition:
Worldliness (Weltlichkeit) refers to the condition of Dasein being-in-the-world and its belongingness to the context of the world.

Quotations:

- "The "there" is essentially constitutive for the worldliness of the world." (From "Basic Concepts")

- "The worldliness of the world lies in the fact that in the world, and as world, entities as entities are encountered." (From "Basic Concepts")

- "Worldliness is the existential determination of that wherein the world as world consists." (From "Basic Concepts"

THE END

Printed in Great Britain
by Amazon